Fortune-Telling by Playing Cards

By Astra Cielo

Copyright © 2020 Lamp of Trismegistus. All rights reserved. No part of this publication may be reproduced or transmitted in any form or by any means, electronic or mechanical, including photocopying, recording, or by any information storage and retrieval system, without permission in writing from Lamp of Trismegistus. Reviewers may quote brief passages.

ISBN: 978-1-63118-467-3

Esoteric Classics

Other Books in this Series and Related Titles

Fortune-Telling with Dice by Astra Cielo (978-1-63118-466-6)

History, Analysis and Secret Tradition of the Tarot
by Manly P. Hall, A. E. Waite &c (978-1-63118-445-1)

Dreams and Their Interpretation by Astra Cielo (978-1-63118-468-0)

Crystal Vision Through Crystal Gazing by Achad (978-1-63118-455-0)

Magical Essays and Instructions by Florence Farr (978-1-63118-418-5)

Ancient Mysteries and Secret Societies by Hall (978-1-63118-410-9)

The Path of Light: A Manual of Maha-Yana Buddhism
by L. D. Barnett (978-1-63118-471-0)

The Rosicrucian Chemical Marriage
by Christian Rosenkreuz (978-1-63118-458-1)

Ghosts in Solid Form by Gambier Bolton (978-1-63118-469-7)

American Indian Freemasonry by A. C. Parker (978-1-63118-460-4)

The Mysteries of Freemasonry & the Druids
by Albert G. Mackey, Manly P. Hall &c (978-1-63118-444-4)

The Legend of the Holy Grail and its Connection with Templars and Freemasons by A. E. Waite (978-1-63118-462-8)

Arcane Formulas or Mental Alchemy
by William Walker Atkinson (978-1-63118-459-8)

The Machinery of the Mind by Dion Fortune (978-1-63118-451-2)

The Gospel of the Nativity of Mary by St. Matthew (978-1-63118-448-2)

Buddhist Psalms by Shinran (978-1-63118-465-9)

Audio Versions are also Available on Audible and iTunes

Table of Contents

Introduction…7

Fortune Telling by Playing Cards

The Origin and History of Playing Cards…9

Telling One's Fortune with Twenty-One Cards
The Italian Method…25
The French System…31
An English System…35
The Gypsy Method…41
The Creole Method…47

Card Oracles…55

INTRODUCTION

The word "esoteric" can be difficult to define. Esotericism in general can be seen less as a system of beliefs and more as a category, which encompasses numerous, different systems of beliefs. It's a bit of juxtaposition, since the word "esoteric" indicates something that few people know about, while the term itself broadly covers numerous philosophies, practices, areas of study and belief systems.

In a greater sense, Esotericism acts as a storehouse for secret knowledge, which is often considered ancient (by *tradition, if not by fact),* passed down from generation to generation, in private. At various times in history, simply possessing the knowledge of some of these subjects, was considered illegal and a jailable offence, if discovered. This usually included such general topics as Alchemy, Qabalah, Hermeticism, Occultism, Ceremonial Magic, Astrology, Divination, Rosicrucianism and so on. Collectively, these areas of study were often referred to as the esoteric sciences.

Sometimes, the outer garment of a subject isn't esoteric, while what is hidden beneath it, is. As an example, Freemasonry isn't necessarily esoteric by nature (at *least not anymore),* but certain signs, passwords and handshakes given to the candidate during their initiation, are in fact, esoteric, in the sense that they are hidden from the general public.

Today, in the twenty-first century, such topics are readily available at bookstores across the country, and numerous mainsteam publishers offer beginners guides and coffee-table volumes on many of these subjects, intended for mass appeal. Books like *"The Secret"* have turned previously arcane topics into household knowledge. All that being the case, however, it isn't to say that there still aren't buried secrets to uncover, ancient wisdom being ignored and forgotten mysteries to be explored. In fact, it is often that we are only able to further our own studies by standing on the shoulders of these disappearing giants.

Lamp of Trismegistus is doing its part to help preserve humanity's esoteric history by making some of these classics available to those students who are seeking to unearth the knowledge of these ancient colossi.

So, be sure to check other titles from our *Esoteric Classics* series, as well as our *Occult Fiction, Theosophical Classics, Foundations of Freemasonry Series, Supernatural Fiction, Paranormal Research Series, Studies in Buddhism* and our *Christian Apocrypha Series*. You can also download the audio versions of most of these titles from iTunes or Audible, for learning on the go.

THE ORIGIN AND HISTORY OF PLAYING CARDS

The history of playing cards extends back five hundred years, and various stories and theories have been mooted as to how and by whom they were first introduced into Europe. Many Eastern nations—notably those of India, China, Chaldea and Egypt—possessed cards for divination and playing purposes which differed both in design and use from those known in Europe at an early date. It seems from ancient manuscripts that the wise men of the East regarded cards with great veneration and ascribed to them mysterious powers. They considered them mediums of revelation from the celestial powers.

Many authorities hold that playing cards were invented by Europeans. It is certain that they were known in Italy as early as 1379, and that the Moors and Saracens introduced them into Spain at an earlier date. The first cards were called "Nabis," and the Hebrew word *"Nabi"* means to prophesy. This gives weight to the theory that the original intention of cards was for purposes of divination.

The earliest cards of which we have any definite knowledge were called "Tarots," which are supposed to have been the invention of a Jewish astrologer and cabalist. Various explanations are given as to the name. The science and divination by means of these cards were supposed to be found in the Egyptian "Book of Thoth," which Moses learned in the Egyptian temples and of which he guarded the secret jealously.

Outside of a few packs in some of the museums, there are no tarot cards to be found. The pictures on them represented priests, popes, jugglers, emperors, devils and other characters. Later on numerals were added to the symbolic cards so that games could be played with them. At the beginning of the fifteenth century, Venice had games of cards composed of 78 cards, 22 containing symbols and 56 numerals. Later the size of the pack was reduced to 52 cards.

Suits and Symbols

There have always been four suits in use, but the symbols used had varied in different countries. Originally they were cups, money, swords and clubs. These are still retained in Italian and Spanish cards. Old German cards have acorns, leaves, hearts and bells. The French cards used spades and clubs, hearts and diamonds. The word "spade" comes from the Italian word meaning a sword. The club sign was adopted from the three-leaf clover. Many of the packs used last century were very costly and artistic. They were painted by hand to represent historic characters.

Mystic Meaning

To many people a pack of cards comes next in importance to the Bible. To others they are supposed to be the devil's own handbooks of destruction. They have exercised an irresistible fascination over the minds of men and women of all ages. A great interest attaches to the many possible combinations to be made from the cards in a pack. It has been pointed out that—

The fifty-two cards represent the 52 weeks in the year.

Thirteen cards in each suit represent the 13 lunar months, and the 13 weeks in each quarter.

The four suits represent the four seasons of the year.

The twelve court cards represent the 12 signs of the Zodiac.

Number of pips on all the plain cards =	220
Number of pips on the court cards =	12
Counting each of the court cards as 10 =	120
Number of cards in each suit =	<u>13</u>
Total equals the number of days in the year	365

The Charm and Power of Cards

We have nothing to do in this book with cards used for gambling purposes, but as instruments of Cartomancy we find them full of charm and interest. Every person has a certain amount of superstition in his nature and desires to take a look into the dim and mysterious future. No one need be ashamed of confessing a certain amount of interest in the unseen and occult. Strange coincidences are happening all the time, and there are many inexplicable occurrences that meet us at every turn. Educated men and women are taking an interest in the occult to a greater extent than ever before, although in the past the great statesmen and famous women of France, even the great Napoleon himself, were believers in the power of cards to foretell the future. Divination by cards is of great antiquity and is still as popular as ever. Formerly it was connected with astrologers' incantation and religious practices. Now, however, it is indulged in principally as a means of amusement. Of course no one need be warned against the danger of taking a pack of cards as a guide in matters of importance requiring judgment and discretion.

What the Cards Signify

There are several systems of telling fortunes by cards. In each the meaning of the cards and the mode of laying them out differ. The meaning of a card is modified when the card is reversed. As our modern packs are practically the same, looking at them from either end, it is well to mark the cards so that you can tell which is the top and which is the bottom. This could be done before starting to use the pack.

Meaning of the Various Cards

Hearts are especially connected with the work of Cupid and Hymen. The suit has also close reference to affairs of the home and to both the domestic and social sides of life.

Diamonds are representative of financial matters, small and great, with a generally favorable signification.

Clubs stand for prosperity, a happy home life with intelligent pleasures and successful undertakings.

Spades forebode evil. They speak of sickness, death, monetary losses and anxieties, separation from friends and dear ones. They are also representative of love, appealing exclusively to the senses.

Meaning of the Hearts

Ace.—A love letter, good news; (reversed) a removal or a visit from a friend.

King.—Fair man of generous disposition; (reversed) a disappointing person.

Queen.—Fair, good-natured woman; (reversed) she has had an unhappy love affair.

Knave.—A young bachelor devoted to enjoyment; (reversed) a military lover with a grievance.

Ten.—Antidote to bad cards, happiness and success; (reversed) passing worries.

Nine.—The wish card, good luck; (reversed) short sorrow.

Eight.—Thoughts of marriage, affections of a fair person; (reversed) unresponsiveness.

Seven.—Calm, content; (reversed) boredom, satiety.

Meaning of the Diamonds

Ace.—A letter, an offer of marriage; (reversed) evil tidings.

King.—A very fair or white-haired man; a soldier by profession, and of a deceitful turn of mind; (reversed) a treacherous schemer.

Queen.—A fair woman, given to gossip and wanting in refinement; (reversed) a rather spiteful flirt.

Knave.—Subordinate official, who is untrustworthy; (reversed) a mischief-maker.

Ten.—Traveling or a removal; (reversed) ill luck will attend the step.

Nine.—Vexation, hindrances; (reversed) domestic wrangling, or disagreement between lovers.

Eight.—Love passages; (reversed) blighted affections.

Seven.—Unkindly chaff, cynicism; (reversed) stupid and unfounded slander.

Meaning of the Clubs

Ace.—Good luck, letters or papers relating to money, pleasant tidings; (reversed) short-lived happiness, a tiresome correspondence.

King.—A dark man, warm-hearted and true as a friend, straight in his dealings; (reversed) good intentions frustrated.

Queen.—A dark woman, loving but hasty, and bearing no malice; (reversed) harassed by jealousy.

Knave.—A ready-witted young man, clever at his work and ardent in his love; (reversed) irresponsible and fickle.

Ten.—Prosperity and luxury; (reversed) a sea voyage.

Nine.—An unlooked-for inheritance, money acquired under a will; (reversed) a small, friendly gift.

Eight.—Love of a dark man or woman which, if accepted and reciprocated, will bring joy and well-being; (reversed) an unworthy affection calculated to cause trouble.

Seven.—Trifling financial matters; (reversed) money troubles.

Meaning of the Spades

Ace.—Emotional enjoyment; (reversed) news of a death, sorrow.

King.—A widower, an unscrupulous lawyer, impossible as a friend, and dangerous as an enemy; (reversed) the desire to work evil without the power.

Queen.—Widow, a very dark woman; (reversed) an intriguing, spiteful woman.

Knave.—Legal or medical student, wanting in refinement of mind and manners; (reversed) a treacherous character, fond of underhand measures.

Ten.—Grief, loss of freedom; (reversed) passing trouble or illness.

Nine.—A bad omen, news of failure or death; (reversed) loss of one near and dear by death.

Eight.—Coming illness; (reversed) an engagement canceled or a rejected proposal, dissipation.

Seven.—Everyday worries, or a resolve taken; (reversed) silly stratagems in love-making.

Combinations of Court Cards

Four Aces.—When these fall together they imply danger, financial loss, separation from friends, love troubles. The evil is mitigated in proportion to the number of them that are reversed.

Three Aces.—Passing troubles relieved by good news, faithlessness of a lover. If reversed, they mean foolish excess.

Two Aces.—These mean union: if Hearts and Clubs, it will be for good; if Diamonds and Spades, for evil, probably the outcome of jealousy. If reversed, the object of the union will fail.

Four Kings.—Honors, preferment, good appointments. If reversed, the good things will be of less value, but will arrive earlier.

Three Kings.—Serious matters will be taken in hand with the best result, unless any of the three cards be reversed, when it will be doubtful.

Two Kings.—Co-operation in business, upright conduct, and prudent enterprises to be crowned with success. Each one reversed represents an obstacle. Both reversed spell failure.

Four Queens.—A social gathering which may be spoilt by one or more being reversed.

Three Queens.—Friendly visits. If reversed, scandal, gossip and possibly bodily danger.

Two Queens.—Interchanged, secrets betrayed, a meeting between friends. When both are reversed, there will be suffering for the inquirer resulting from his own acts. Only one reversed, means rivalry.

Four Knaves.—Jolly conviviality. Any of them reversed lessens the evil.

Three Knaves.—Worries and vexations from acquaintances, slander calling the inquirer's honor in question. If reversed, it foretells a passage-at-arms with a social inferior.

Two Knaves.—Loss of goods. If both are reversed, the trouble is imminent; if one only, it is near.

Combinations of Plain Cards

Four Tens.—Good fortune, success. The more there are reversed, the greater number of obstacles in the way.

Three Tens.—Ruin brought about by lawsuits. When reversed, the evil is decreased.

Two Tens.—Unexpected luck, which may be connected with a change of occupation. If one be reversed, it will come soon; if both are reversed, it is distant.

Four Nines.—Unexpected events. The number that are reversed stand for the time to elapse.

Three Nines.—Health, wealth and happiness. If reversed, it means financial difficulties caused by imprudence.

Two Nines.—Prosperity and contentment accompanied by business matters. If reversed, small worries.

Four Eights.—Attending a journey or the taking up of a new position. If reversed, undisturbed stability.

Three Eights.—Thoughts of love and marriage, new family ties. If reversed, flirtation and foolishness.

Two Eights.—Pleasures and passing love fancies. If reversed, disappointments.

Four Sevens.—Schemes and contention and opposition. If reversed, failure of same.

Three Sevens.—Loss of friends, ill-health, remorse. If reversed, slight ailments or unpleasant reaction.

Two Sevens.—Mutual love and marriage. If reversed, faithlessness or regret.

General Information

When a number of court cards fall together it is a sign of hospitality, festive social intercourse, and gaiety of all kinds.

Married people who seek to read the cards must represent their own life partner by the king or queen of the suit they have chosen for themselves, regardless of anything else. For example, a very dark man, the King of Spades, must consider his wife represented by the Queen of Spades.

Bachelors and spinsters may choose cards to personate their lovers and friends.

A court card placed between two cards of the same grade—for instance, two nines, two sevens, etc.—shows that the one represented by that card is threatened.

Should a military man consult the cards he must always be represented by the King of Diamonds.

It is always essential to cut cards with the left hand, there being a long-established idea that it is more intimately connected with the heart than the right. A round table is generally preferred by those who are in the habit of practicing cartomancy. It is a matter of opinion as to whether the cards speak with the same clearness and accuracy when consulted by the inquirer without a fortune-teller. The services of an expert are generally supposed to be of great advantage, even when people have mastered the rudiments of cartomancy themselves.

TELLING ONE'S FORTUNE WITH TWENTY-ONE CARDS

THE ITALIAN METHOD

Thirty-two cards are actually required for this method, although only 21 of them are used. After shuffling the cards and cutting with the left hand, the fortune-teller counts off the first 11 cards and lays them aside. From the 21 which are left he takes the top card and lays it apart, then he lays out the other 20 on the table before him. One card must represent the inquirer, either a knave or a queen, according to the sex. If this card is not among the 20 cards on the table the pack must be dealt over. The meaning of the cards must then be considered; if any set of 2, 3 or more of a kind occur their meaning should be read also, as it may modify the general interpretation of the rest. The 20 cards should be read from left to right continuously to let each card continue the meaning of the one before. The cards must then be put together again and shuffled and cut as before. The top card is again laid aside and the others divided into 3 packs, of which 2 contain 7 cards each and the last only 6 cards. The inquirer chooses one of the packs, which is next turned with the face up and one after the other the cards are to be read according to their significance. This operation must be repeated 3 times.

The following will give an example of how these cards are to be manipulated:

Let us take the Knave of Clubs as representing the inquirer, and the 21 cards selected are the following in their regular order: King of Spades, Queen of Hearts (reversed), Ace of Hearts, Knave of Clubs, Ace of Spades (reversed), Ace of Clubs, Knave of Hearts, King of Hearts, Queen of Spades (reversed), Nine of Hearts, Knave of Diamonds, Ten of Spades, Ace of Diamonds (reversed), King of Diamonds, Seven of Diamonds, Eight of Diamonds, Eight of Spades (reversed), Seven of Clubs (reversed), Nine of Clubs (reversed), Nine of Diamonds. The Surprise placed apart.

On examining this list carefully we find there are 4 Aces, which indicate danger and financial loss. The fact that one of them is reversed shows that the trouble is somewhat lightened.

There are 3 Kings, which indicate that important matters will be undertaken and carried thru successfully by the inquirer.

There are 2 Queens, both reversed, which show that the young man may suffer thru his own faults.

There are 3 Knaves, which mean more worries and vexations thru which the inquirer's honor may be at stake.

Three Nines, however, are indicative of happiness and wealth, although there will be difficulties to overcome.

The 2 Eights indicate some love interest and flirtation.

And the 2 Sevens speak of mutual love and marriage, although one being reversed adds an element of regret.

We will now follow the cards as they lie before us from left to right:

The King of Spades is an unscrupulous man who is a dangerous enemy and will cause trouble.

The Queen of Hearts, reversed, speaks of a woman who, while good-natured, has had an unlucky love affair and on whom the inquirer has set his heart.

The Ace of Hearts indicates that a love letter containing good news will be sent to her by the inquirer.

The Knave of Clubs, a clever young fellow, is mixed up in the affair, but some grief may affect his health as indicated by the Ace of Spades, while the Ace of Clubs, coming immediately after, shows that this sorrow may have something to do with money matters.

The 3 court cards which follow are indicative of a good time in which the inquirer will have to deal with the Knave of Hearts, who is a young bachelor devoted to enjoyments, the King of Hearts a man of generous disposition, and the Queen of Spades, reversed, a dark, intriguing woman.

The Nine of Hearts shows that the inquirer will have good luck and pleasure, but the Knave of Diamonds, following immediately after, shows that an untrustworthy friend is trying to bring him to trouble.

The Ten of Spades means considerable worry and is followed by the Ace of Diamonds, reversed, which also indicates bad tidings in which the King of Diamonds, an old soldier with a deceitful turn of mind and who has a grievance against the inquirer, will have recourse to scandal and slander, as indicated by the Seven of Diamonds.

Next comes the Eight of Diamonds, which shows that the inquirer will indulge in love-making, but he is in for considerable worry as his offer of marriage will be rejected.

The Seven of Clubs tells him that money matters will also cause worry until the Nine of Clubs, reversed, indicates that a gift of money will relieve the situation somewhat. However, there will still be vexatious hindrances, as indicated by the Nine of Diamonds.

The "Surprise" may now be turned up, and contains, let us say, the King of Clubs—a warm-hearted, true friend, straight in his dealings, thru whom happiness and prosperity may come to the inquirer.

The Significance of the Three Packs

As before stated, after having read these cards as a continuous message, the cards must be again shuffled and cut into three packs. The inquirer is asked to choose one of the packs. We will take it for granted that he takes the middle pack, containing 7 cards. Let us say, for example, that this pack contains the following cards: Knave of Diamonds, Seven of Diamonds, Ace of Clubs, Queen of Spades (reversed), Ace of Spades, Ace of Diamonds, Eight of Diamonds. Reading these cards, we notice three Aces, which indicate a lot of trouble—possibly a faithless lover—to be followed by good news. The Knave of Diamonds, an untrustworthy friend mixed up in a scandal which is shown by the Seven of Diamonds, and is brought about by a letter relating to money, as shown by the Ace of Clubs. A widow with an intriguing mind, shown by the Queen of Spades, has something to do in this trouble. The Ace of Spades foretells enjoyment—probably an offer of marriage or a letter, as indicated by the Ace of Diamonds. The Eight of Diamonds foretells a happy marriage after all these troubles.

The inquirer now selects another pack, which is to be read in the same manner, and finally the third pack is to be similarly interpreted.

THE FRENCH SYSTEM

Thirty-two cards are required, rejecting all under the Sevens. They must be shuffled and cut as usual and divided into two packs of 16 each. The inquirer chooses one of the packs, and the first card is laid aside for the "Surprise." The remaining 15 cards are turned face upward and laid on the table from left to right. A certain card must be selected to represent the inquirer. And this must be in the pack he selects. If not, the division must be gone over again until this card is found in the selected pack.

Method of Reading

If there are any 2, 3 or 4 of a kind their explanation must first be given. Next start from the card representing the inquirer and count in groups of 7 from right to left. Next, pair the end cards together and read their meaning. After this shuffle the 15 cards again and divide them into three packs of 5 cards each. The top card of each is first removed and placed with the other which has been set apart as the "Surprise." This will leave three packs of 4 cards each. Inquirer then chooses one of the packs, and the 4 cards are laid out on the table from left to right and their meaning is read. The left-hand pack is "for the house," the right-hand pack "for those who do not expect," and the remaining pack is "for the surprise."

Let us suppose, for example, that the inquirer, being a woman, is represented by the Queen of Clubs. She chooses the middle of the three packs, which contains the Knave of Clubs, Eight of Diamonds (reversed), Eight of Hearts, Queen of Clubs. These will be read as follows: "A clever young man is ardent in his love and is flirting with the inquirer. He has thoughts of marriage in which the inquirer plays a very important part. And the prospects are favorable."

The next pack, which is "for the house," may have the following cards: Knave of Spades, Ace of Spades, Knave of Hearts, King of Spades. They are read as follows: There are 3 Spades, which indicate disappointment. Two Knaves coming together indicate loss of goods and other trouble. The Knave of Spades indicates a legal gentleman of not very refined character who is employed by his master, an unscrupulous lawyer, as shown by the King of Spades, and who is an enemy of the inquirer. A young bachelor devoted to pleasure, however, will help the inquirer out of difficulty. The next pack, which is for "those who do not expect," is, we will say, composed of the Queen of Hearts, Ten of Spades, Ace of Clubs, Nine of Clubs. These indicate that a fair-haired lady, who has had considerable grief, will bring letters relating to money to the inquirer, possibly an unlooked-for inheritance which will change the career of the inquirer. In the case of a merchant, it may mean new customers.

Finally comes the pack "The Surprise," in which we will find The Ace of Hearts, Queen of Spades, Nine of Diamonds, Ten of Hearts. These are read as follows: "A love letter with the best of news will be received. A dark-haired lady will throw hindrances and trouble into the path of the inquirer, in spite of which happiness and success will be the final outcome."

AN ENGLISH SYSTEM OF TELLING THE PAST, PRESENT AND FUTURE

We will present an easy and generally accepted method of telling fortunes by means of cards. Thirty-two cards are required, which are shuffled and cut in the usual way. After being cut, the top card of the lower pack and the bottom card of the upper pack are laid aside and form the "Surprise," then the packs are placed one upon the other. This leaves 30 cards, which are dealt into three equal parts; the pack at the left representing the *past*, the one in the middle the *present*, and the one to the right the *future*.

The man or woman wishing to know what Fortune has in store is called the "Inquirer"; he is represented by a card (supposing him to be a man) which we will say is the Knave of Hearts. Let us now suppose that the ten cards representing the *past* are as follows:

>Ace of Clubs (reversed)
>
>King of Spades
>
>Knave of Diamonds
>
>King of Clubs
>
>Nine of Hearts
>
>Ten of Spades
>
>Seven of Spades (reversed)

Eight of Spades (reversed)

Seven of Clubs

Nine of Clubs

If we refer to the meaning of the cards as already given, we will find the following as to the man's past:

The Ace of Clubs shows that happiness has been of short duration.

The King of Spades denotes that an unscrupulous friend has been at work.

The Knave of Diamonds shows that this man has been a mischief-maker.

The King of Clubs indicates that a warm heart and true friend have been of considerable assistance.

The Nine of Hearts shows that this man has brought good luck.

The Ten of Spades indicates that there has been considerable grief and some loss of freedom due to circumstances over which the inquirer had no control.

The Seven of Spades (reversed) shows that silly love-making has cast its influence over the inquirer.

The Eight of Spades (reversed) shows, however, that the engagement has been canceled or rejected.

The Seven of Clubs indicates that trifling financial matters have at times made life sorrowful.

The Nine of Clubs indicates that this financial condition will be solved by an unlooked-for inheritance.

The next pack being in the center represents the *present*, and we find, perhaps, that the cards run as follows:

        Ace of Diamonds

        Ten of Diamonds

        Knave of Hearts (reversed)

        King of Hearts (reversed)

        Seven of Diamonds

        Nine of Spades

        Eight of Hearts

        Queen of Hearts

        Seven of Hearts

        Queen of Diamonds (reversed)

The reading of the cards will be as follows:

The Ace of Diamonds denotes the coming of an offer of marriage or a letter.

The Ten of Diamonds, following immediately after, indicates that the letter is about a voyage or a removal.

This is followed by the Knave of Hearts, and indicates that it is a question of a young bachelor who is devoted to enjoyment.

Being followed by the King of Hearts (reversed), it indicates that his dealings with the inquirer will be very disappointing.

The Seven of Diamonds, which follows, explains that the inquirer will come in for considerable unkindly chaff.

The Nine of Spades (reversed) foretells a loss of one that is near and dear, thru death.

The Eight of Hearts, which follows, tells that the inquirer is harboring an affection for a fair lady. She is revealed to us in the Queen of Hearts as a good-natured, lovable woman who, according to the Seven of Hearts, is quietly and contentedly awaiting developments.

The Queen of Diamonds (reversed) tells him to beware of a woman who is a spiteful flirt and apt to make trouble.

The third pack represents the *future*, and we have the following cards:

> Queen of Clubs
>
> King of Diamonds
>
> Eight of Diamonds
>
> Ten of Clubs
>
> Nine of Diamonds

Eight of Clubs

Ace of Diamonds (reversed)

Ace of Hearts (reversed)

Knave of Spades (reversed)

Queen of Spades (reversed)

The Queen of Clubs indicates a dark-haired woman, rather loving but apt to cause trouble.

The King of Diamonds is an old man who is also inclined to make mischief.

The Eight of Diamonds shows that there have been some love passages between the inquirer and the lady which may develop into a romance, which, according to the Ten of Clubs, promises to be prosperous.

The Nine of Diamonds, however, shows that all will not be smooth sailing, for, according to the Eighth of Clubs, a dark-haired man is also paying attention to this woman and may make headway in his attentions.

According to the Ace of Diamonds (reversed) the inquirer must be prepared for evil tidings.

The Ace of Hearts (reversed) foretells a visit from a friend, which the Knave of Spades (reversed) shows is a medical student, not of the most refined character.

The Queen of Spades (reversed) shows that an unscrupulous and spiteful woman is weaving her spell around the inquirer, and he had better beware.

Again examining the cards of the *future*, we find two Queens, one reversed, which means rivalry between the women influencing this fortune. There are also two Eights, which indicate intrigue and opposition.

This is but a brief summary of the way in which this method is worked. A great deal depends, of course, upon the cleverness of the fortune-teller in interpreting the cards according to the disposition of the inquirer.

THE GYPSY METHOD

A very simple method, especially when there are many fortunes to be told, which is often used by the Romany folks, is the following. In this method the meanings are somewhat different from those given in previous chapters. These new meanings may better suit the characteristics of the inquirer, and in connection with the readings already given they add many facts of importance.

Thirty-two cards are taken, the numbers under 7 being thrown out. The cards are shuffled and cut into three packs by the inquirer, each pack being turned face up. The center pack is taken first, then the one to the right, finally the one to the left, and placed upon each other in this position. The fortune-teller holds this newly arranged pack in his left hand and takes off 3 cards facing upwards, selecting the highest card of any suit that may appear. He retains this one and lays the others aside for the next deal. Continue doing this until the pack is finished. Then shuffle all the discarded cards together, until you have 21 cards or more on the table. If 3 cards of any suit appear, or 3 cards of the same value, they must all be taken.

A card must now be selected to represent the inquirer. If she be fair of complexion she selects Diamonds; if medium fair, Hearts; if of brown hair, she selects Clubs; and if very dark, Spades. A man selects the King and a woman the Queen. This representative card is shuffled with the others and taken out when it is the highest of its suit. Should there be 21 or more cards selected before it appears, then it must be taken from the remainder and placed last of all.

The cards are read from left to right, and are placed in horseshoe shape as they are drawn out. Picture cards represent people, and the number of spots relates to money or events. Diamonds concern themselves with money and interest; Hearts, with love affairs and affection; Clubs, with business events; and Spades, with the more serious affairs of life.

The following gives the significance of each card:

Hearts

King	A fair man
Queen	A woman of similar complexion
Knave	An honest friend
Ten	A wedding
Nine	A wish
Eight	Love
Seven	Friendship
Ace	Home.

Diamonds

King	A fair man
Queen	A fair woman
Knave	A companion
Ten	A wealthy marriage
Nine	Rise in social position
Eight	Success thru speculation
Seven	A good income
Ace	A present.

Clubs

King	A man of medium complexion
Queen	A woman
Knave	A successful friend
Ten	A trip by water
Nine	Successful business
Eight	Social pleasure
Seven	A business affair
Ace	A letter or legal document.

Spades

King	A dark man
Queen	A dark woman (or widow)
Knave	Thoughts of personal matters
Ten	A journey by land
Nine	Sorrow or sickness
Eight	A loss of money or friends
Seven	A quarrel.

Three Kings coming together indicate a new friend; a Knave and 2 Kings, meeting an old friend; 3 Knaves, business at law; 3 Queens, a quarrel with a woman; 3 Tens, a lucky deal. If the Ten of Hearts, Ten of Clubs and Ten of Diamonds come together, it means that a wealthy marriage will follow a journey across the sea. Three Nines indicate good news; 3 Eights, a removal; 3 Sevens, unsatisfactory news; 3 Aces, very good luck. An Ace of Clubs and of Diamonds together, a letter which will bring an offer of marriage. The Ace and Nine of Hearts indicate that a desire will be realized at home; the Ace and Nine of Spades foretell death and sorrow in your family; the King, Queen and Ten of any suit mean that you will hear of a marriage soon.

Reading the Cards

Let us now take a typical example of this method. Let the inquirer be represented by the Queen of Hearts. Shuffle and divide the pack into 3, giving the King, Knave and Seven of Hearts, indicating that the inquirer has a male friend of medium complexion and good intentions. Lay these 3 cards in order beginning with the left hand. The fortune-teller now proceeds to draw off 3 cards, making his selection as above explained. Having finished the pack, he repeats the process twice more. We will suppose that in these deals the following cards have been selected:

King, Knave, Seven of Hearts, Ace of Clubs, King of Spades, Queen of Clubs, Queen of Diamonds, Queen of Spades, King of Clubs, Knave of Diamonds, Ace of Hearts, Knave of Spades, King of Diamonds, Knave of Clubs, Queen of Hearts, Ace of Diamonds, Ten of Hearts, Eight of Clubs, Seven of Spades, Ace of Spades, Ten of Clubs, Ten of Spades and Ten of Diamonds.

Beginning from the Queen of Hearts, as the starting-point, we proceed to count 7 to the left. The seventh card being the Queen of Spades, the seventh from this is the King of Hearts, and again counting to the seventh we get the Ten of Hearts.

This is to be read as follows:

The inquirer has many good friends, but the Queen of Spades represents a woman who will interpose difficulties to her marriage, but without effect. The next card is the Knave of Diamonds followed by the Seven of Hearts and the Seven of Spades; which combination represents news coming soon, but which may not be advantageous to the inquirer. The Knave of Spades is followed by the King and Ten of Clubs, which denotes that a dark man is separated from the inquirer, but thinks of her and hopes to be with her soon.

THE CREOLE METHOD

You will no doubt remember the fascinating story of how Josephine, the wife of Napoleon I. and Empress of France, had her fortune told when still a girl. She was a Creole—that is a native of the West Indies and of French descent. Tradition tells us that she went to an old colored witch, who laid out the cards according to the Creole system and from them prophesied, "You will be greater than a queen." Josephine at first had faith in this prediction, but after waiting for a king to propose to her, she married a French soldier named Beauharnais, by whom she had two children. He died during the early part of the French Revolution. Napoleon, who at that time was a poor lieutenant, deeply in debt and without prospects, proposed to her. He did not seem likely to carry out the prophecy and raise her to be more than queen; so she refused him. At last she was won over by his persistency and married him. In the course of years she became Empress of France.

Just what the Creole method of divination was had been forgotten for many years. The following system, however, has recently been declared by an old gypsy of Martinique to be the exact method used by the fortune-teller of Josephine. It will not be found in any other book. It will be interesting principally because it differs materially from all the methods given in other books on cartomancy.

Begin by shuffling all the 52 cards thoroughly. The inquirer then cuts them and takes the pack in his left hand, first holding it on his forehead and saying, "Que le cerveau parle!" which means, "Let the Brain speak,"—then holding it over the heart, saying, "Que le cœur décide!" or in English, "Let the Heart decide." The operator then takes the cards and spreads them fanwise before her on the table, with the backs up. The inquirer then draws out at random the mystic number of 9 cards, arranging them as follows, face up:

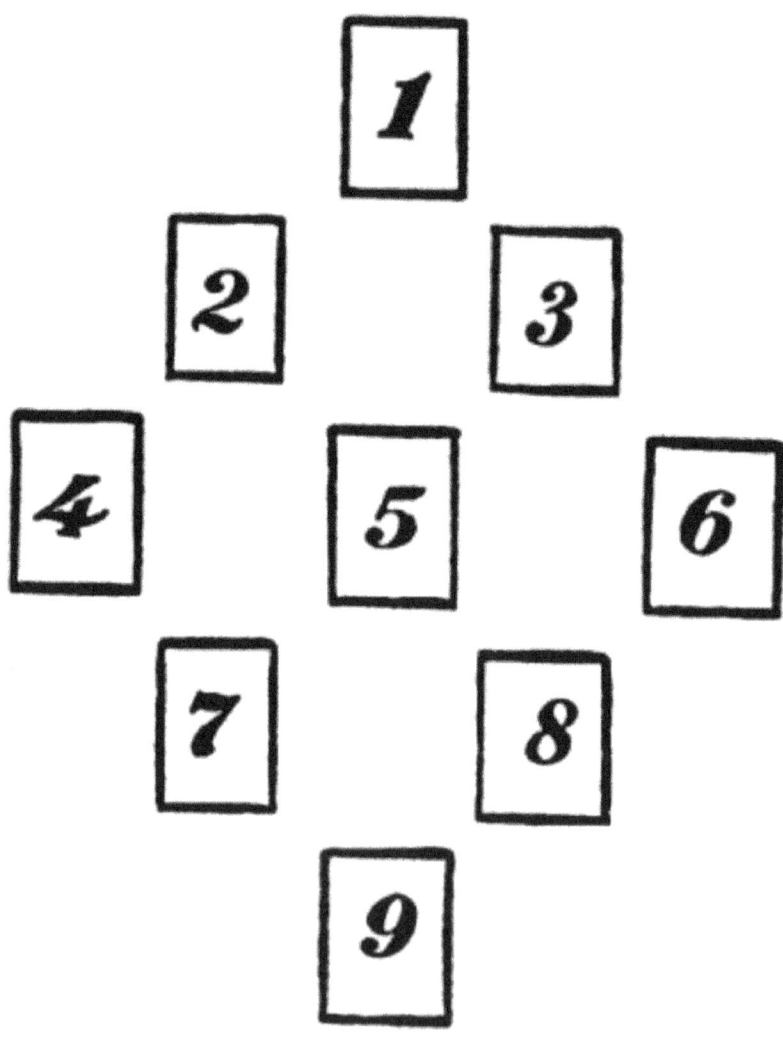

The first card is called the "Key Card," for it decides the interpretation to be put on the rest. If it is a Heart, it foretells the height of success; if a Diamond, it foretells wealth; if a Spade, it brings misfortune; if a Club, it denotes hard work. The next two cards decide the time in which the fortune will be determined. The low spots indicate a short space, the higher spots, a longer space of time. The court cards indicate a remote fortune, but a happy one. The next three cards indicate the rank or station to which Fortune will elevate the inquirer. If court cards, the Fates will be kind; if ordinary or low cards, the inquirer will have to be content with mediocrity. The Ace means disgrace or, at best, a very low station.

The next two cards denote the course of married life. If court cards, the marital relations will be happy; if low cards, there will be trouble and friction, The Ace means unhappiness at home. The last card is devoted to health. A court card means the best of health; the lower, more or less serious illness, according to the degree indicated by their spots. The Ace means an early death. The cards that were drawn by Josephine were (so we are informed):

King of Hearts

Ten of Diamonds   Nine of Diamonds

Queen of Hearts   Queen of Diamonds   Queen of Clubs

King of Diamonds   King of Clubs

Ten of Hearts

It will be seen that every card denotes the height of fortune—a combination that is rarely met with. After reading the mystic nine, the remaining cards are again shuffled and the inquirer draws out thirteen cards at random from the pack. These are arranged in the form of a cross as shown in the diagram.

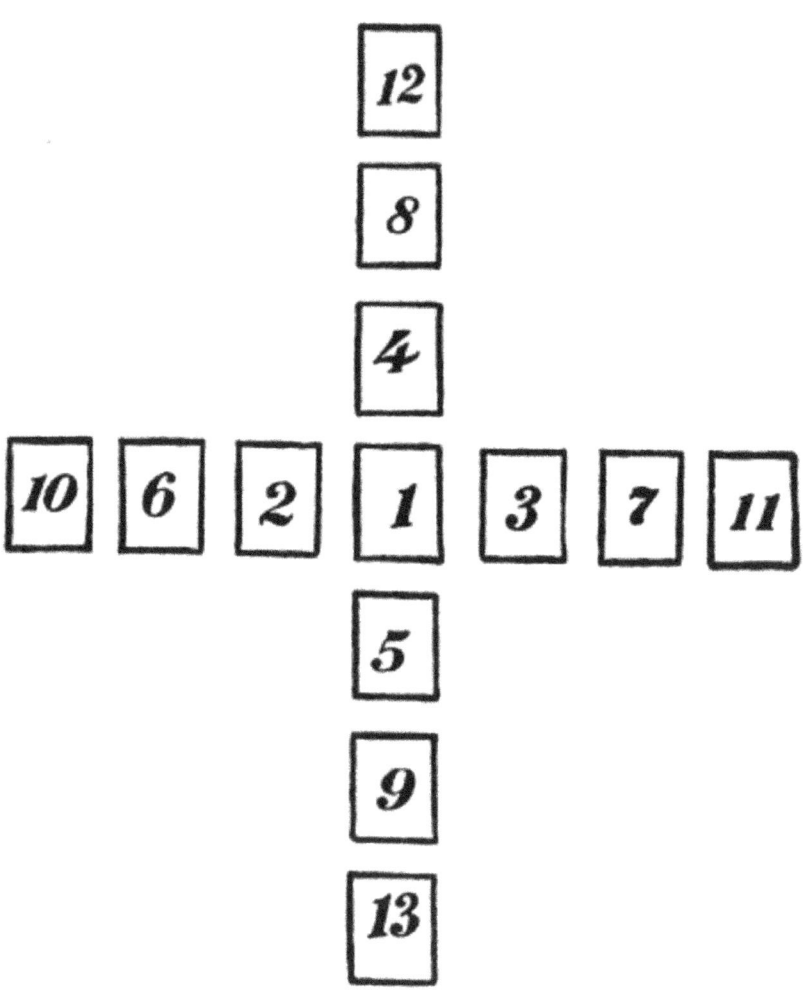

Put the first card in the center and the remaining cards to left, right, top and bottom as indicated by the numbers. The reading of the cards is as follows:

Hearts denote love; Diamonds, wealth; Clubs, hard work; and Spades, misfortune.

Of the court cards, Kings are lucky for women inquirers and Queens for men. Knaves are lucky if red and unlucky if black.

The Ace is always a sign of coming evil.

The odd numbers are lucky for men and unlucky for women, and the even numbers are the reverse. A 2-spot means a gift; a 3-spot, a letter; a 4-spot, news; a 5-spot, an accident; a 6-spot, a change; a 7-spot, friendship; an 8-spot, assistance; a 9-spot, home conditions; a 10-spot, business conditions.

Let us suppose the cards just laid out in a cross are the following:

                        Knave of Hearts
                        Ten of Clubs
                        Ace of Spades
Three of Diamonds   King of Spades
Eight of Hearts   Four of Hearts   Queen of Spades
Ten of Hearts   Four of Hearts
                        Seven of Diamonds
                        Knave of Spades
                        Two of Clubs

This we would read as follows, the inquirer being a lady:

The Knave of Hearts denotes luck in love; probably a suitor if the inquirer be unmarried, or a loving husband if the inquirer be married.

The Ten of Clubs indicates that business conditions will soon improve, for an even number is lucky for ladies. The Ace of Spades shows a very dark and pressing trouble that threatens. Three of Diamonds shows that money will be lost by a foolish transaction. Eight of Hearts shows that fortunate assistance will be at hand. Ten of Hearts means that through friendship the business conditions will have greatly improved.

The King of Spades means that a dark man will have a disagreeable effect upon the inquirer, and the Queen of Spades, the man's wife, will be instrumental in making things unpleasant. Be careful not to get into their bad graces.

The Four of Hearts indicates welcome news from a dear friend. The Seven of Diamonds shows that this friendship will bring gain of money as well. Knave of Spades means, "Beware of a treacherous man who is disposed to do you harm!" The Two of Clubs means an unexpected gift from a business man, or possibly a gain through hard luck. Other interpretations may be put on these cards according to the temperament of the fortune-teller.

A modification of this method is to draw 21 cards instead of 13. Arrange 12 of these in the form of a semicircle, and the other 9 in the form of a triangle within the circle. To discover the past, read the circle first from left to right. Then to predict the future, read the triangle beginning at the left-hand angle, going up to the apex, down on the right-hand side, and across the base.

CARD ORACLES

Answering questions by means of cards is a popular pastime. If the inquirer wishes to know—

"When will my wedding be?"

…she draws four cards and lays them face up on the table. The spots must be counted to get the number of weeks. A Queen or King means a speedy marriage with prosperity. A Knave means a delay. An Ace signifies trouble and bids the inquirer consider well before taking the important step.

"Will my lover be true to me?"

Lay the top 15 cards on the table face up. If the Ten, Nine or Eight of Hearts is among them, the chances are favorable. If the Ace of Spades is among them, the omen is bad. If the King of Hearts turns up, you can trust him for life.

"Have I cause for jealousy?"

Count off the top 9 cards. If the Ace of any suit is among them, beware, for there is someone he loves better than you.

"Shall we ever part?"

Lay out 4 cards from the top in the form of a cross. Count the spots. If odd, then you will never part; if even, be prepared for a short parting in the future. If an Ace is among them, the parting will be a long one.

"Is it advisable for me to change my residence?"

Lay 9 cards in a circle face up. If the middle card is a picture card, remain where you are. If a small card, the number of spots indicate in how many months you should move. If an Ace, it indicates the need of great care.

"What fortune is there in store for me?"

Take off 3 cards and lay them face up. If red cards, they foretell a good fortune; if black, trouble. If a King or Queen appears, it means that influential friends will help. If a Knave, beware of an enemy. If an Ace, you will have a struggle to achieve success.

HEARTS
In days of youth, life's golden spring,
When throbs of love begin;
Then hearts are trumps, and fate will bring
A hand that's sure to win.

DIAMONDS
In summer time of joyous life,
When gifts of wealth expand;
Then diamonds are trumps, and the happy wife
Finds them a winning hand.

CLUBS

In the autumn days of life's decline,
When friends are choice but few;
Then clubs are trumps, and club-life fine
Holds winning hands for you.

SPADES

When winter comes with hoary age,
Then spades are trumps, my boy.
The Sextons spade will close life's page,
With its sorrow and its joy.

www.ingramcontent.com/pod-product-compliance
Lightning Source LLC
LaVergne TN
LVHW041459070426
835507LV00009B/704